Copyright © 2016 Sweary Animals

Swear Word Coloring Book

All Rights Reserved Worldwide

Swear Word
Adult Coloring Book
Deep In The Rude Rude Woods
(Sweary Animals)

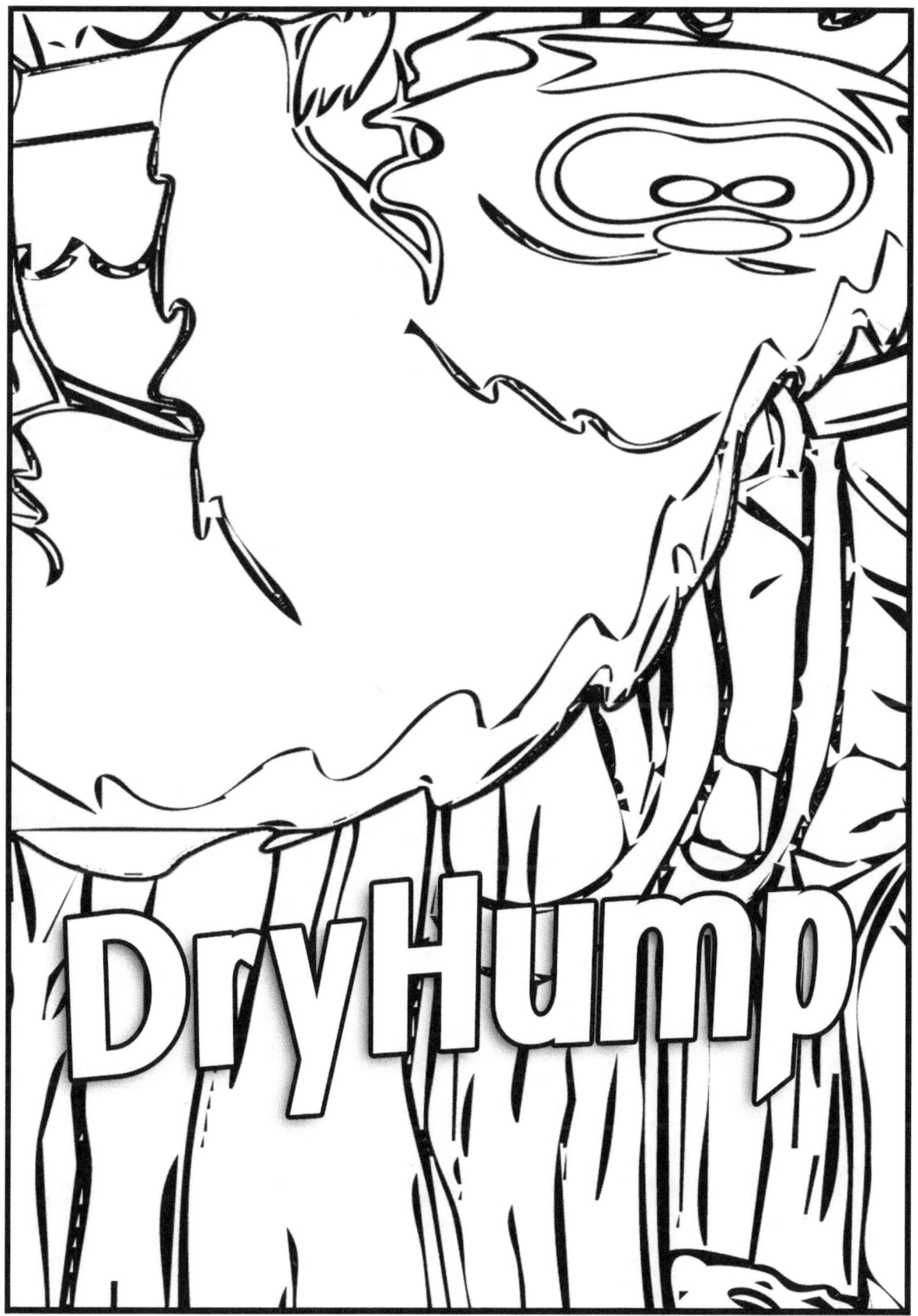

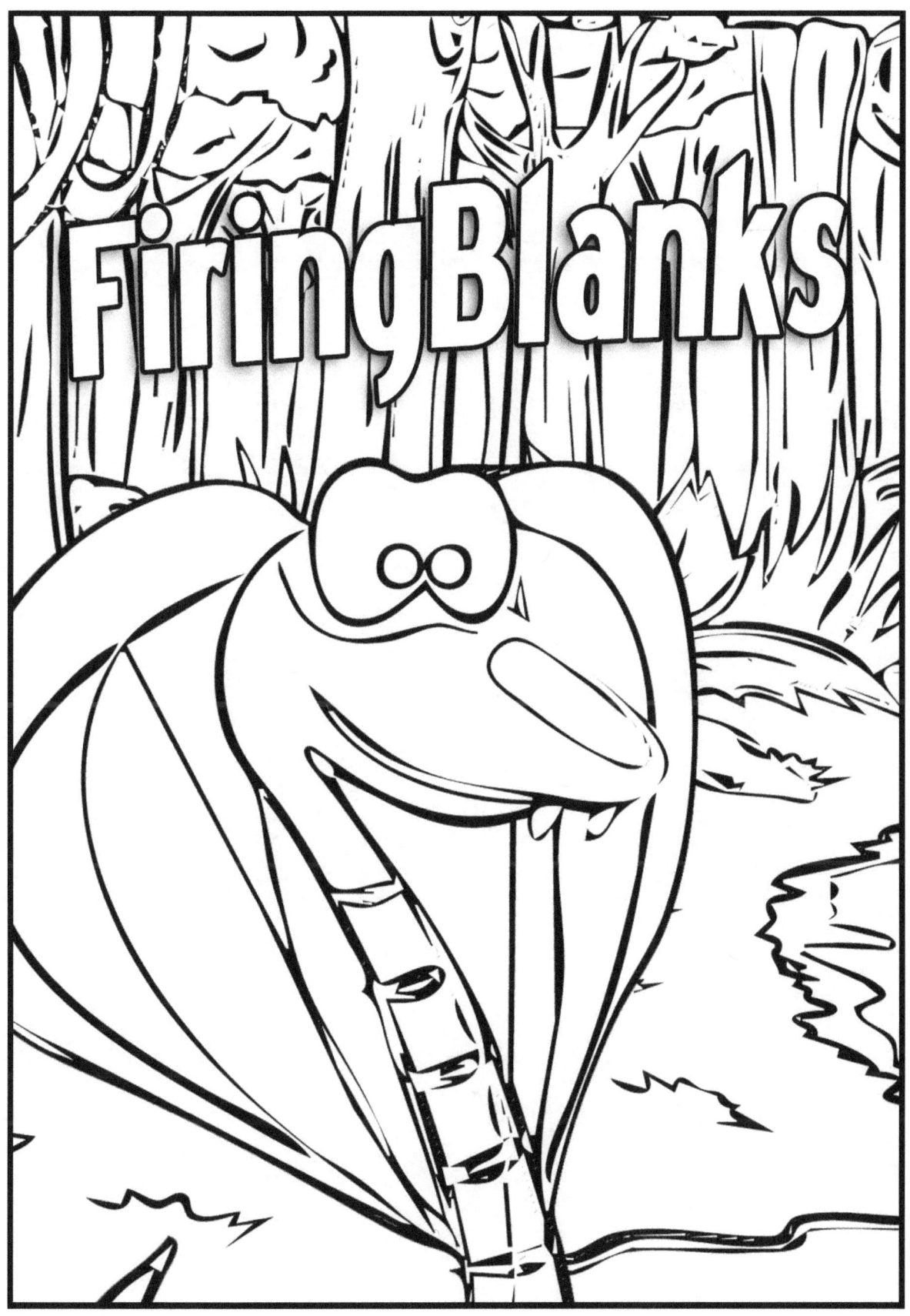

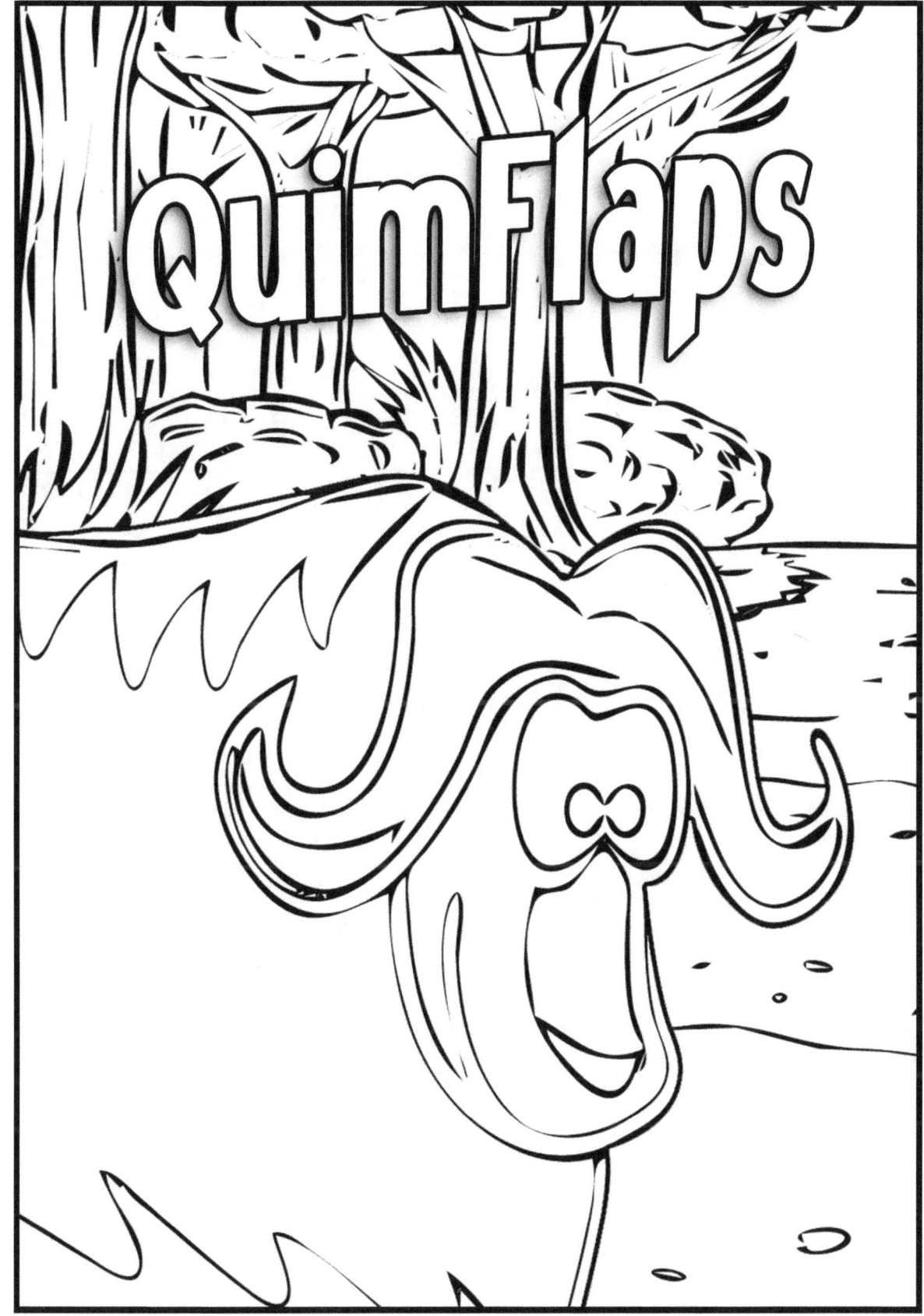

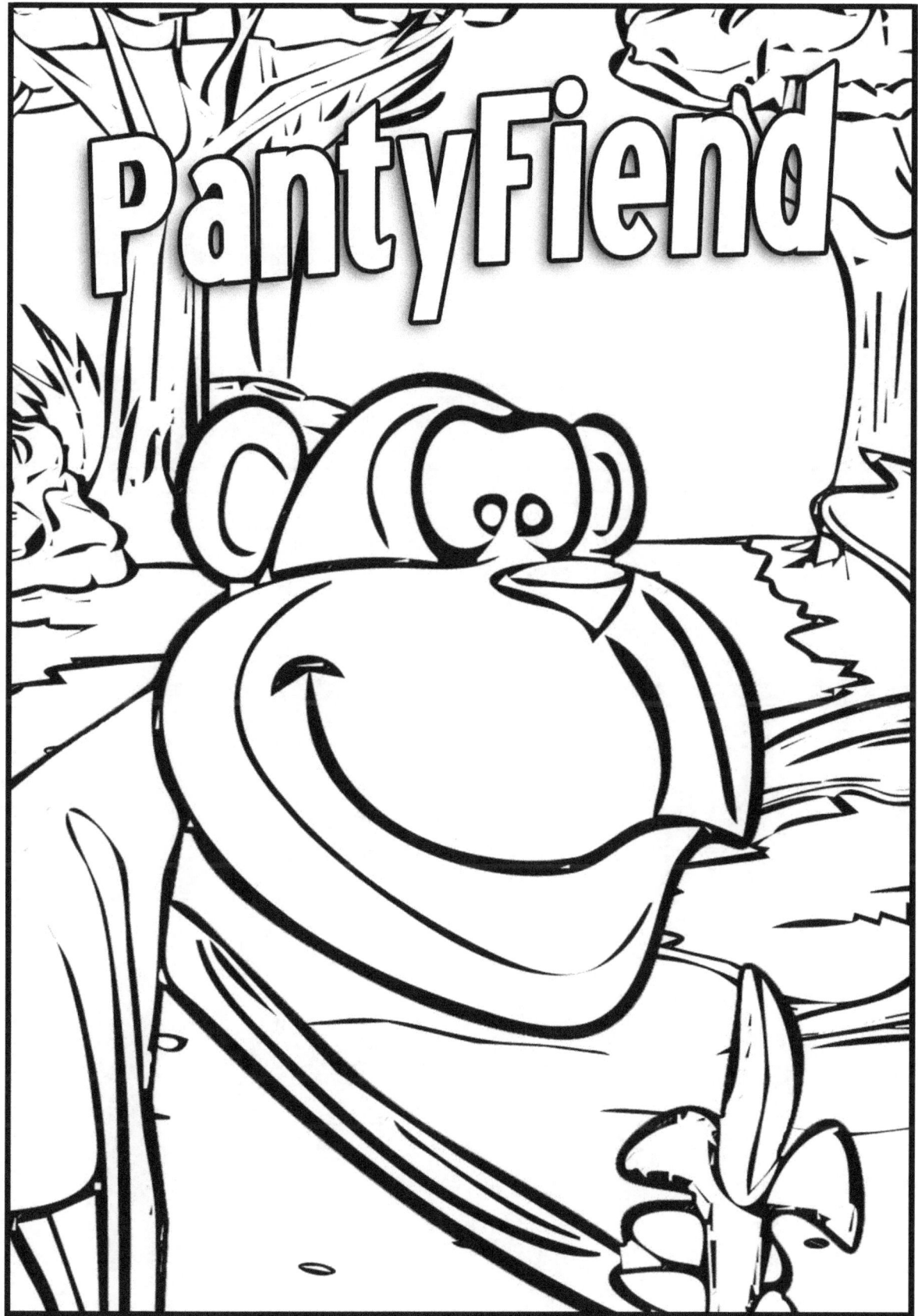

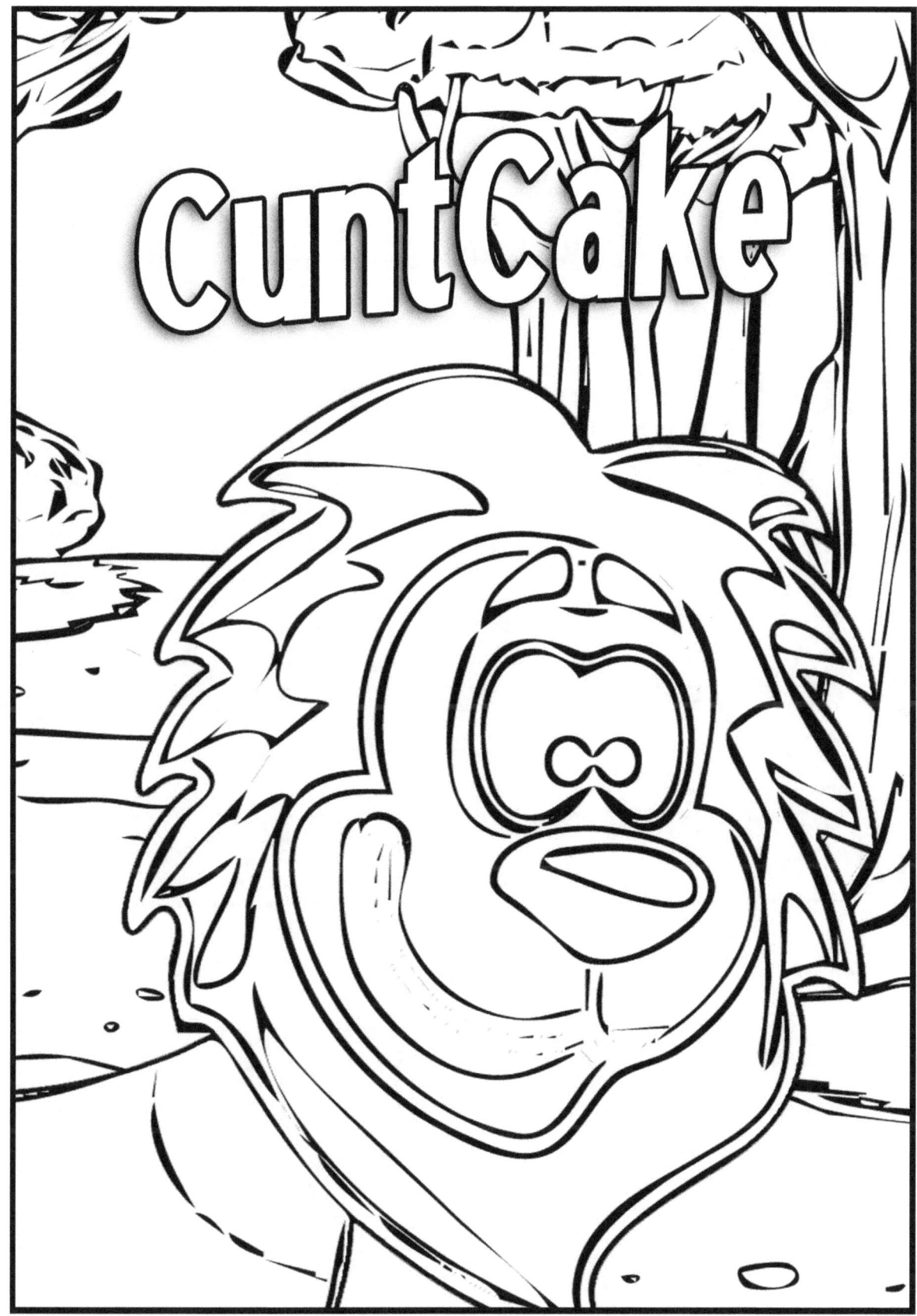

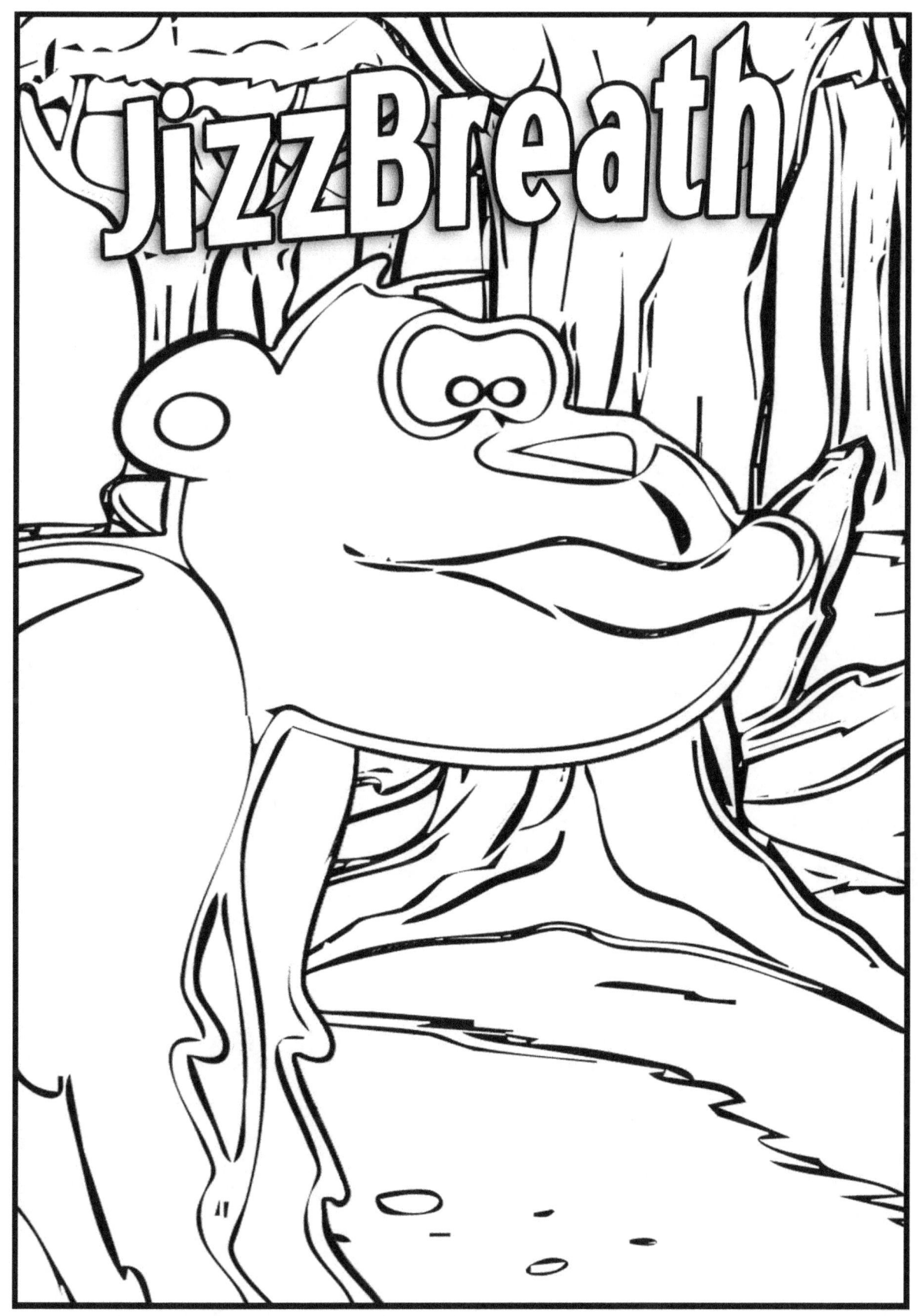

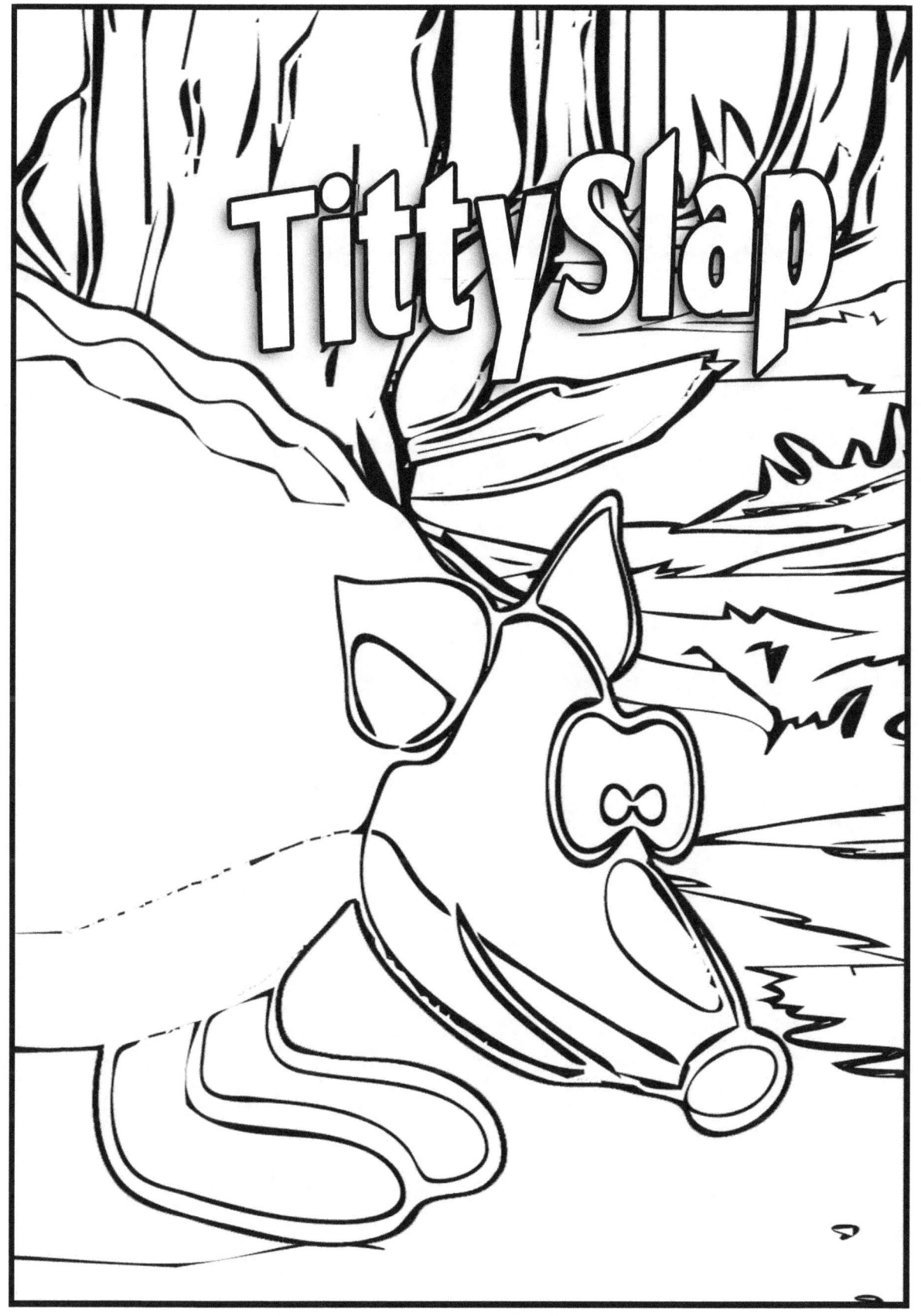

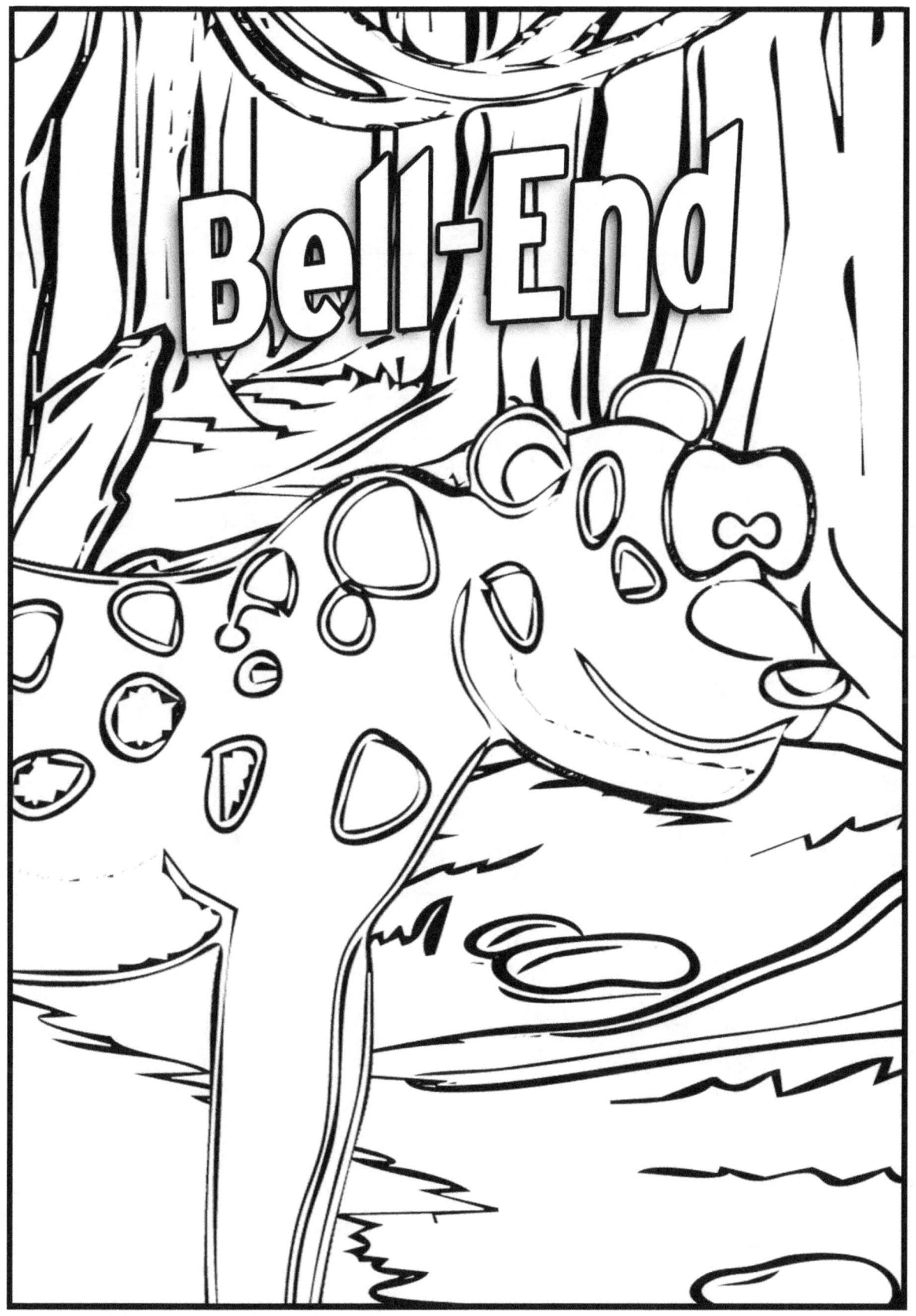

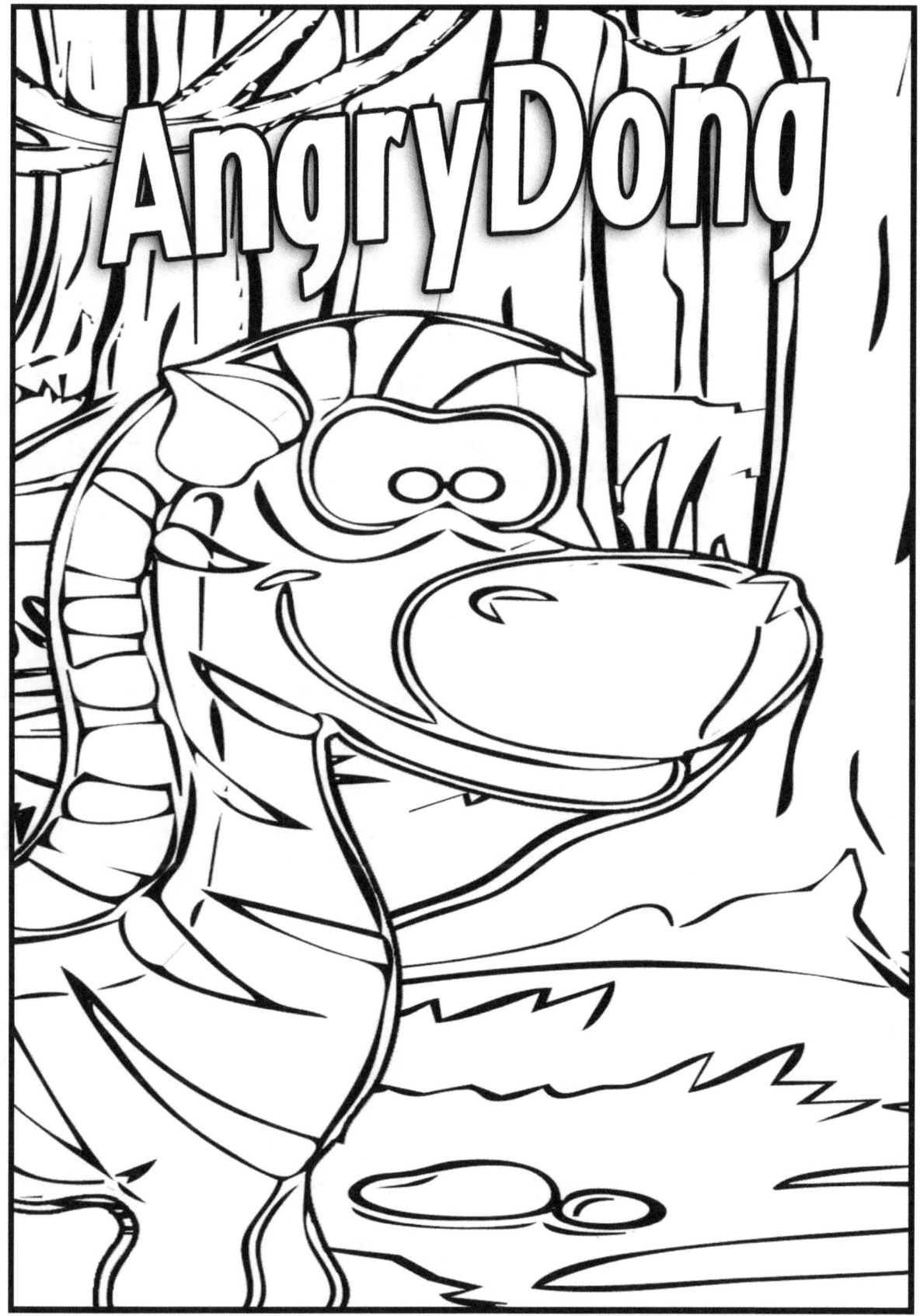

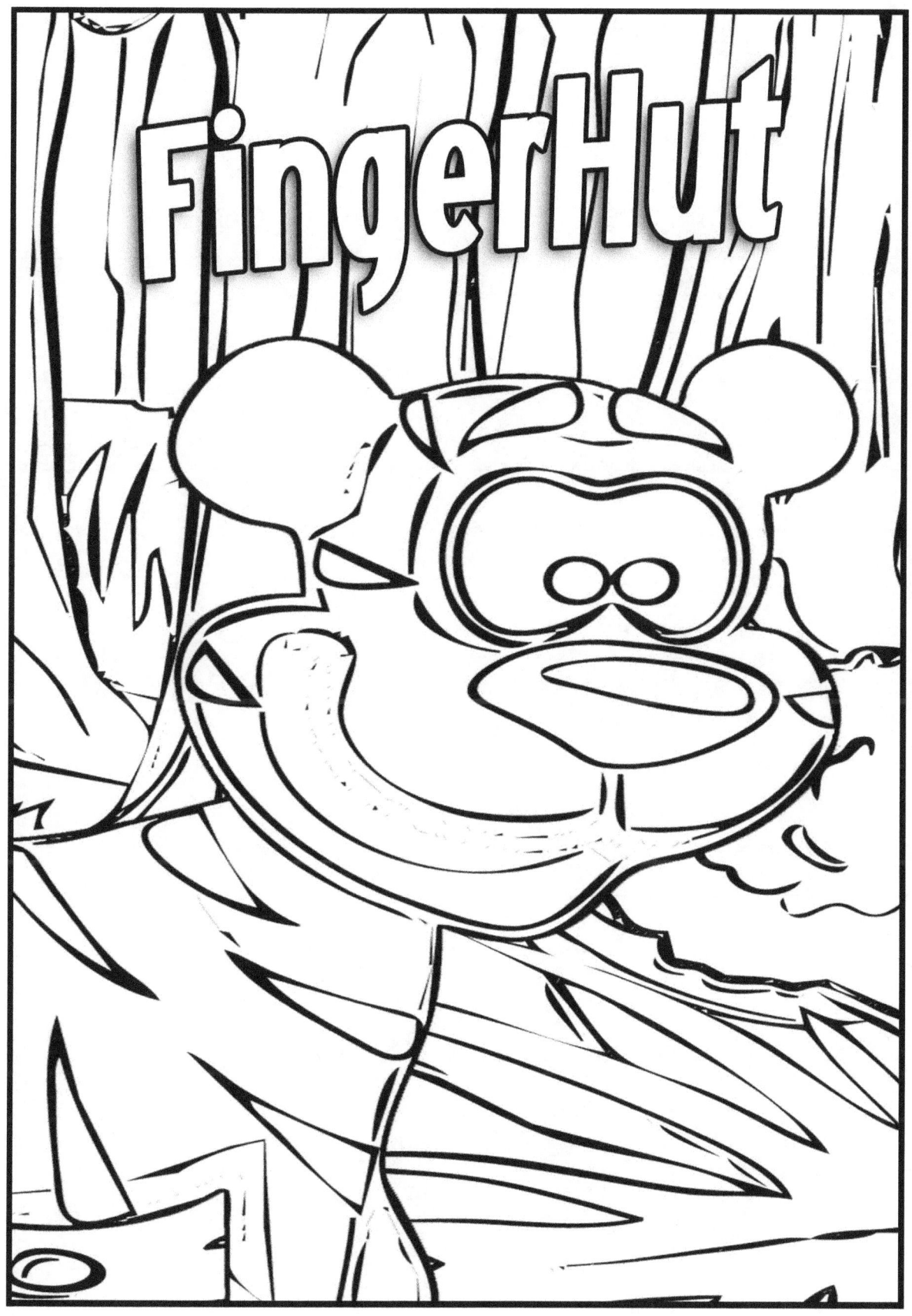

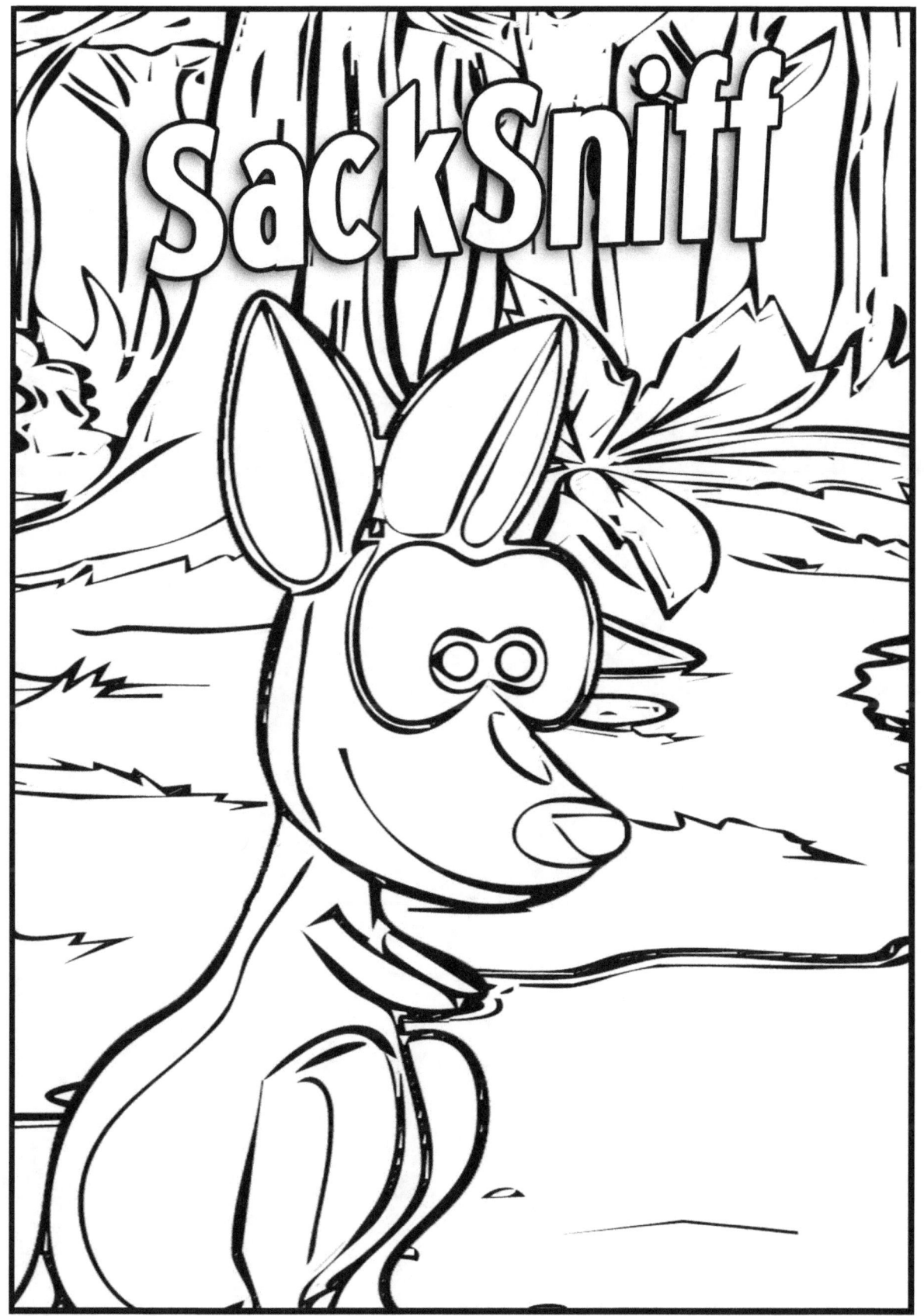

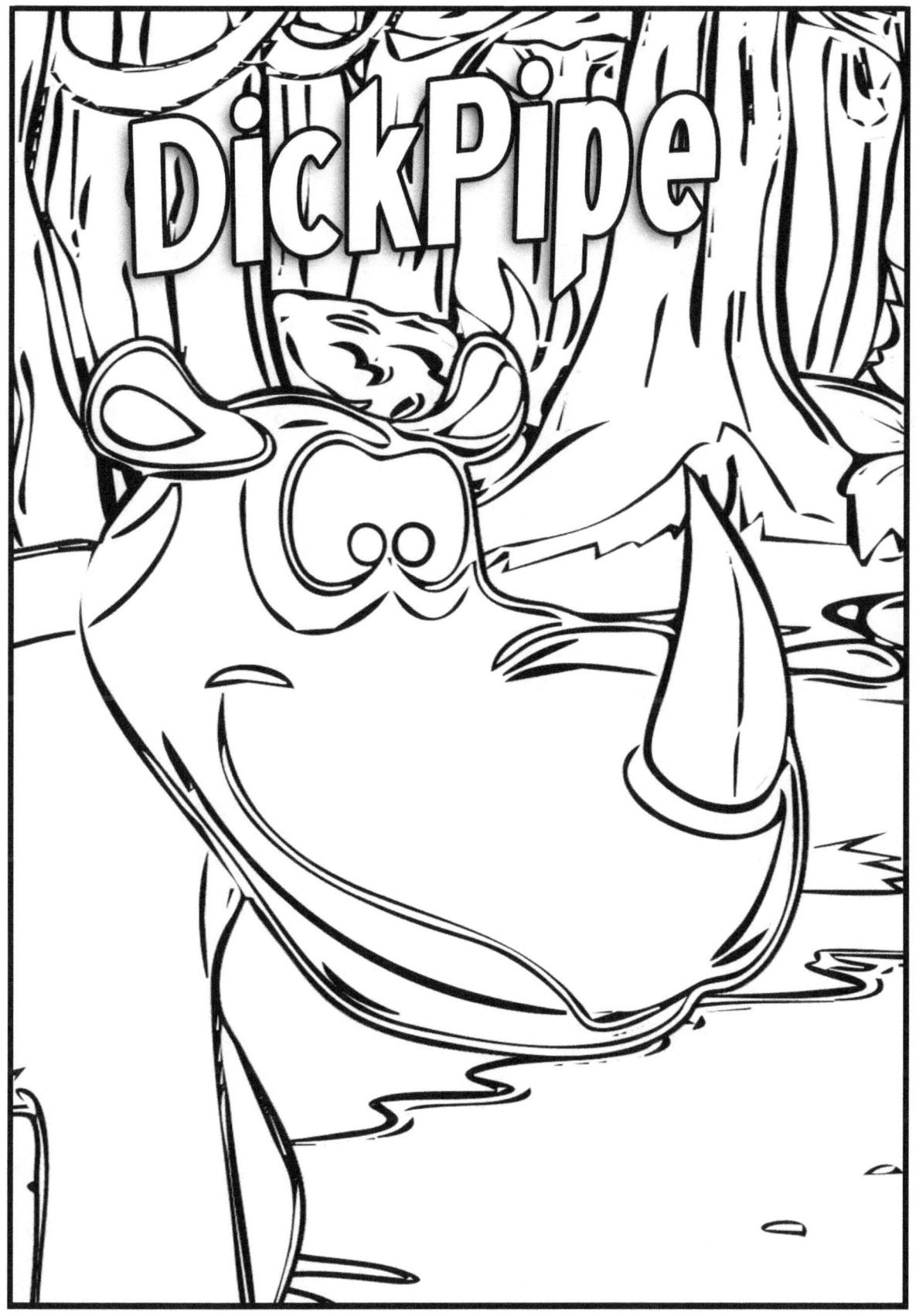

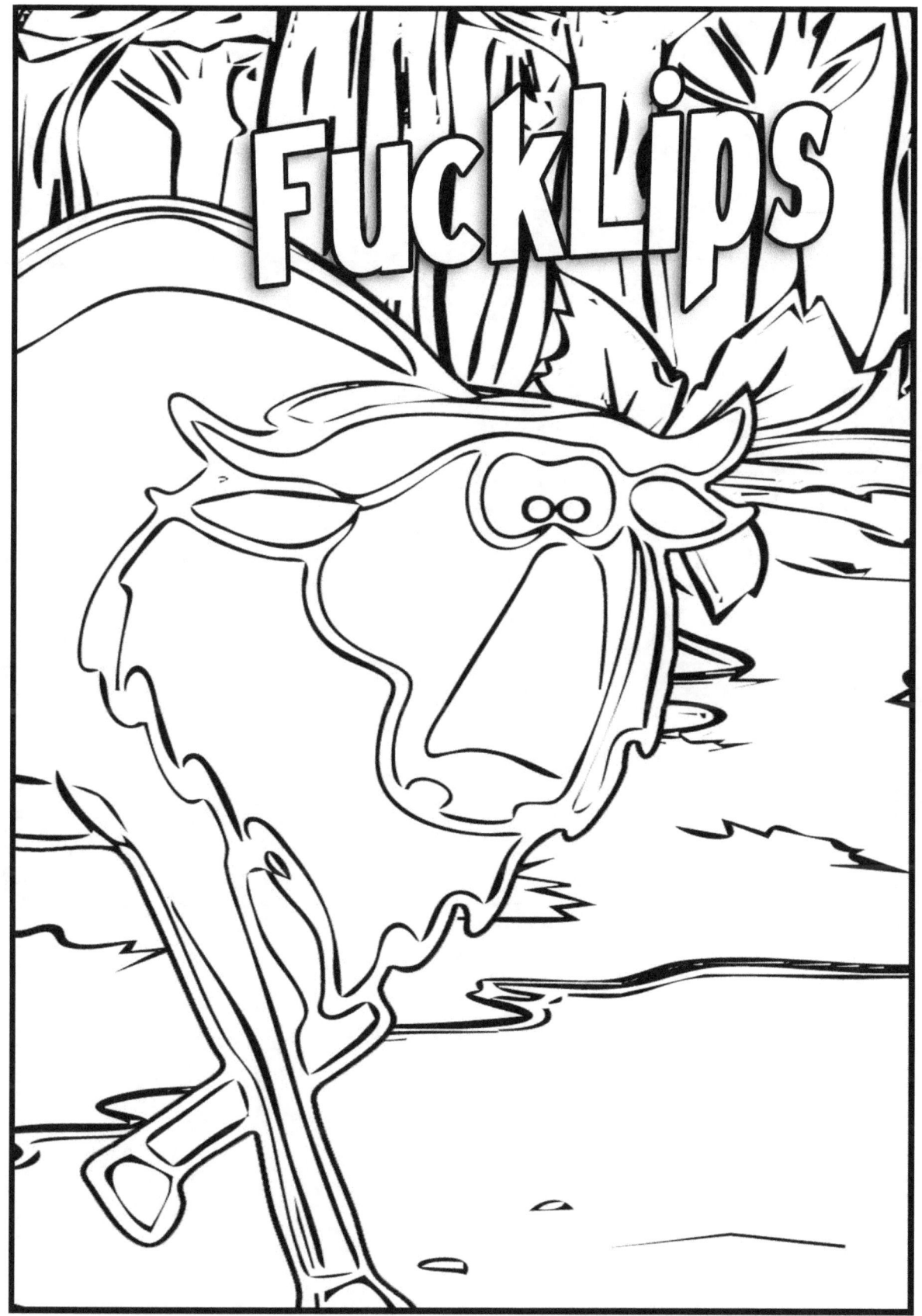

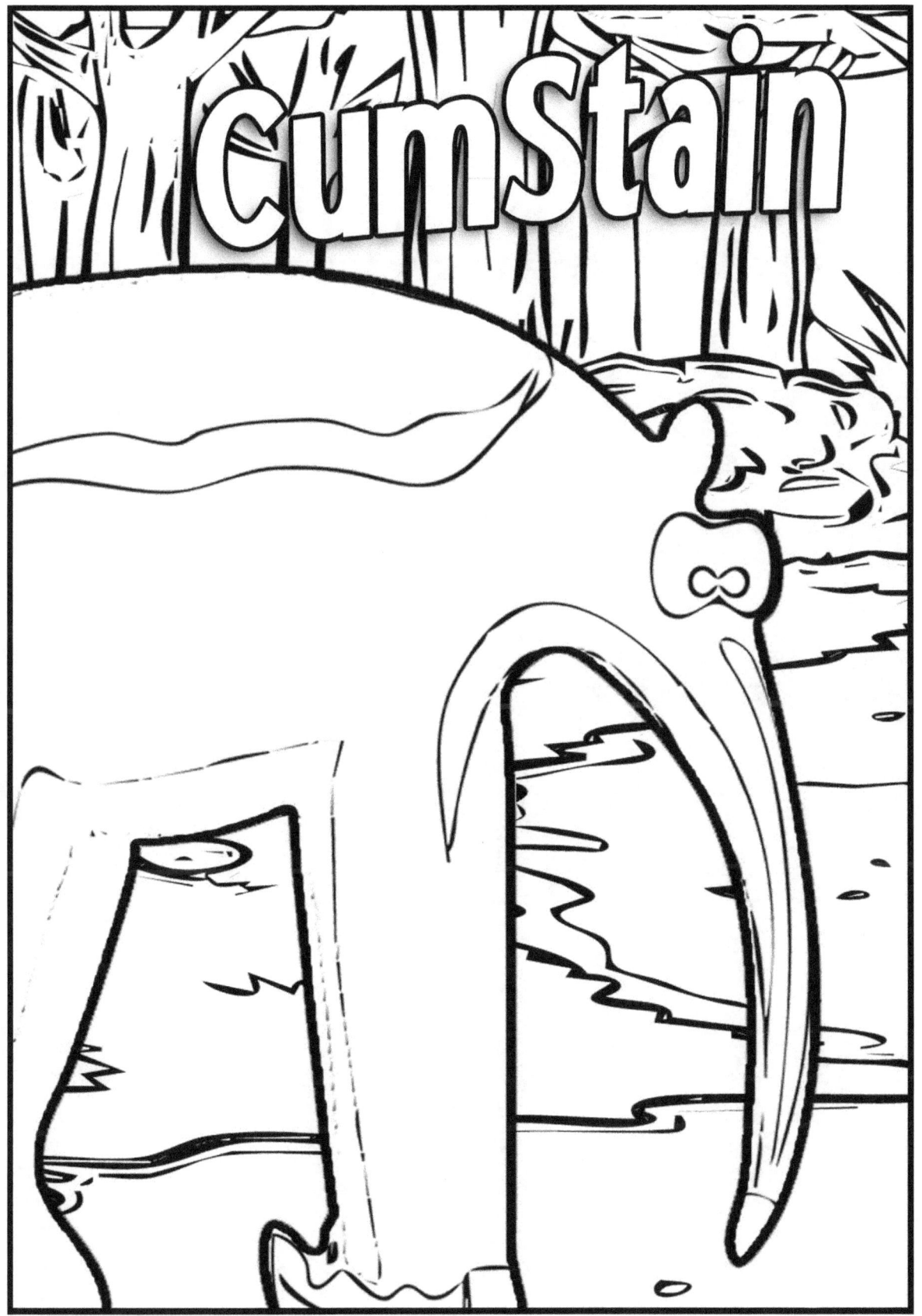

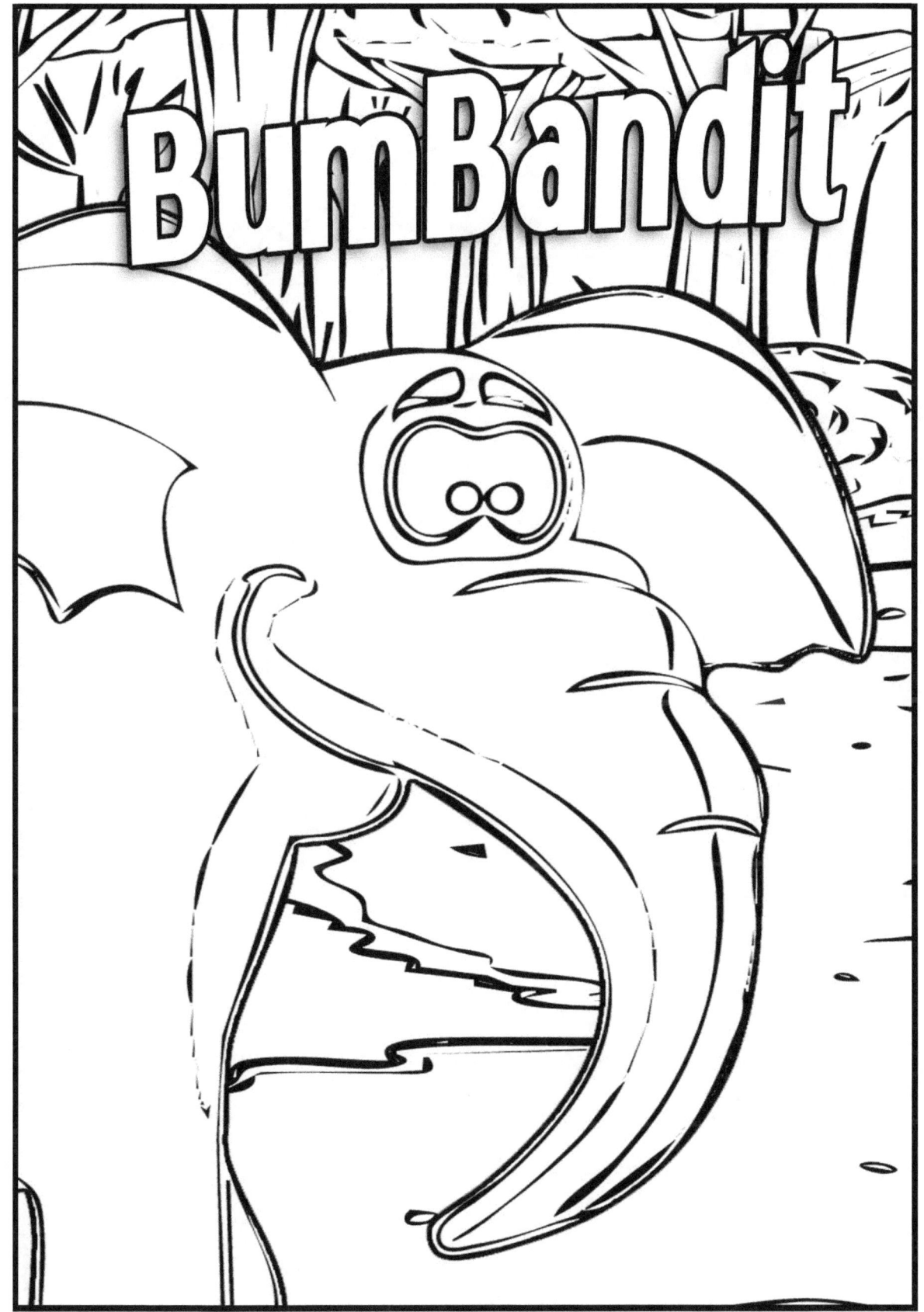

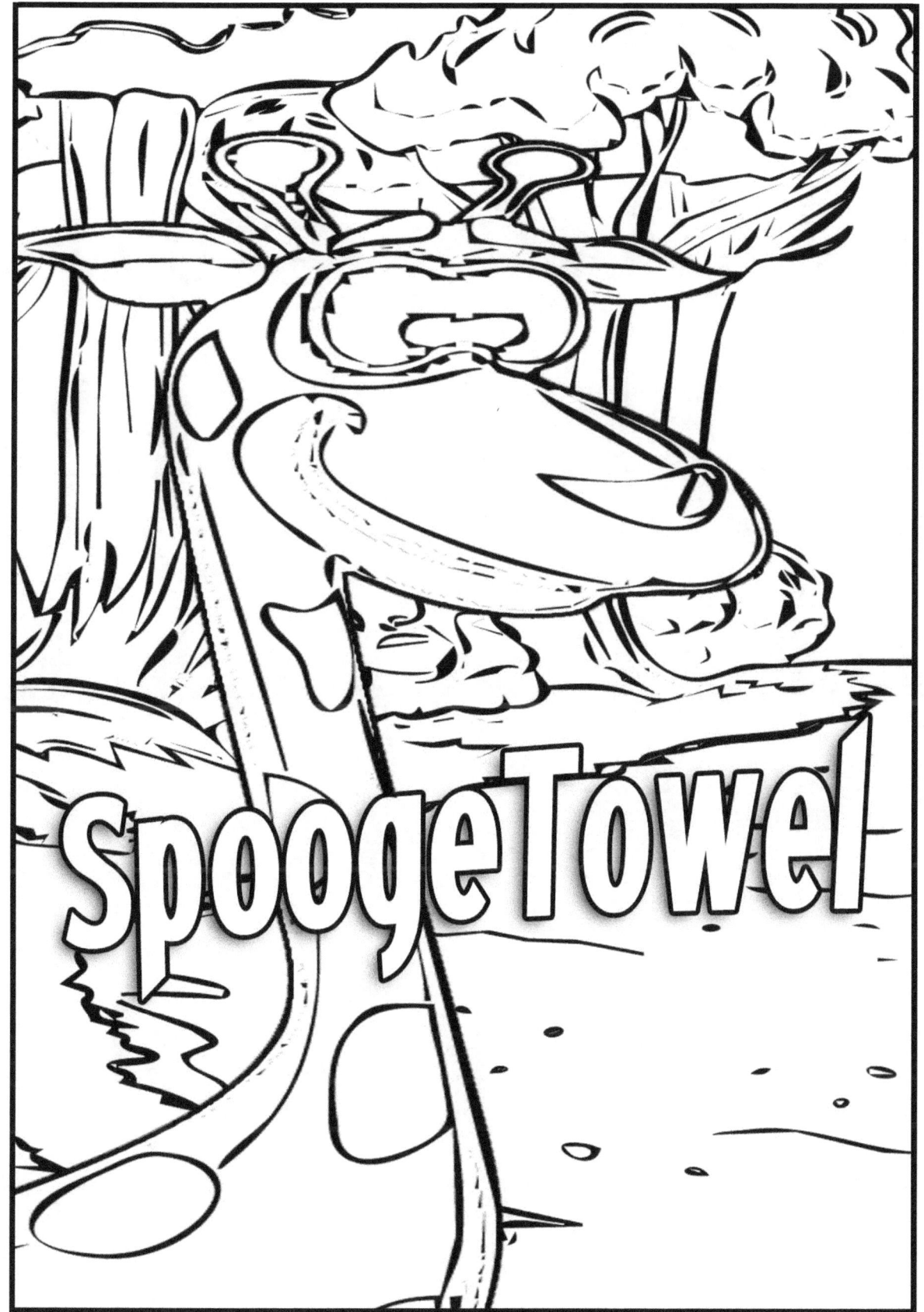

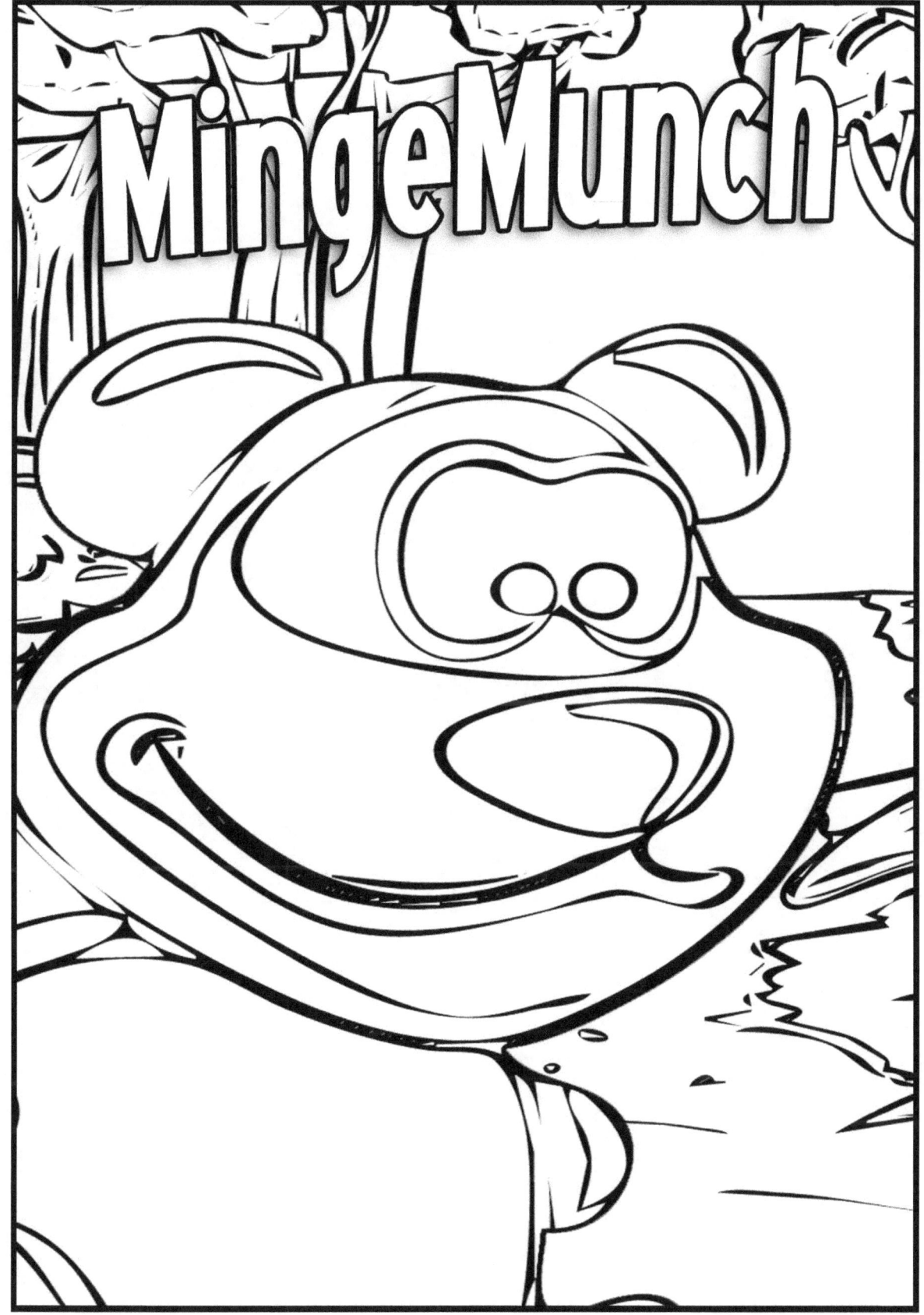

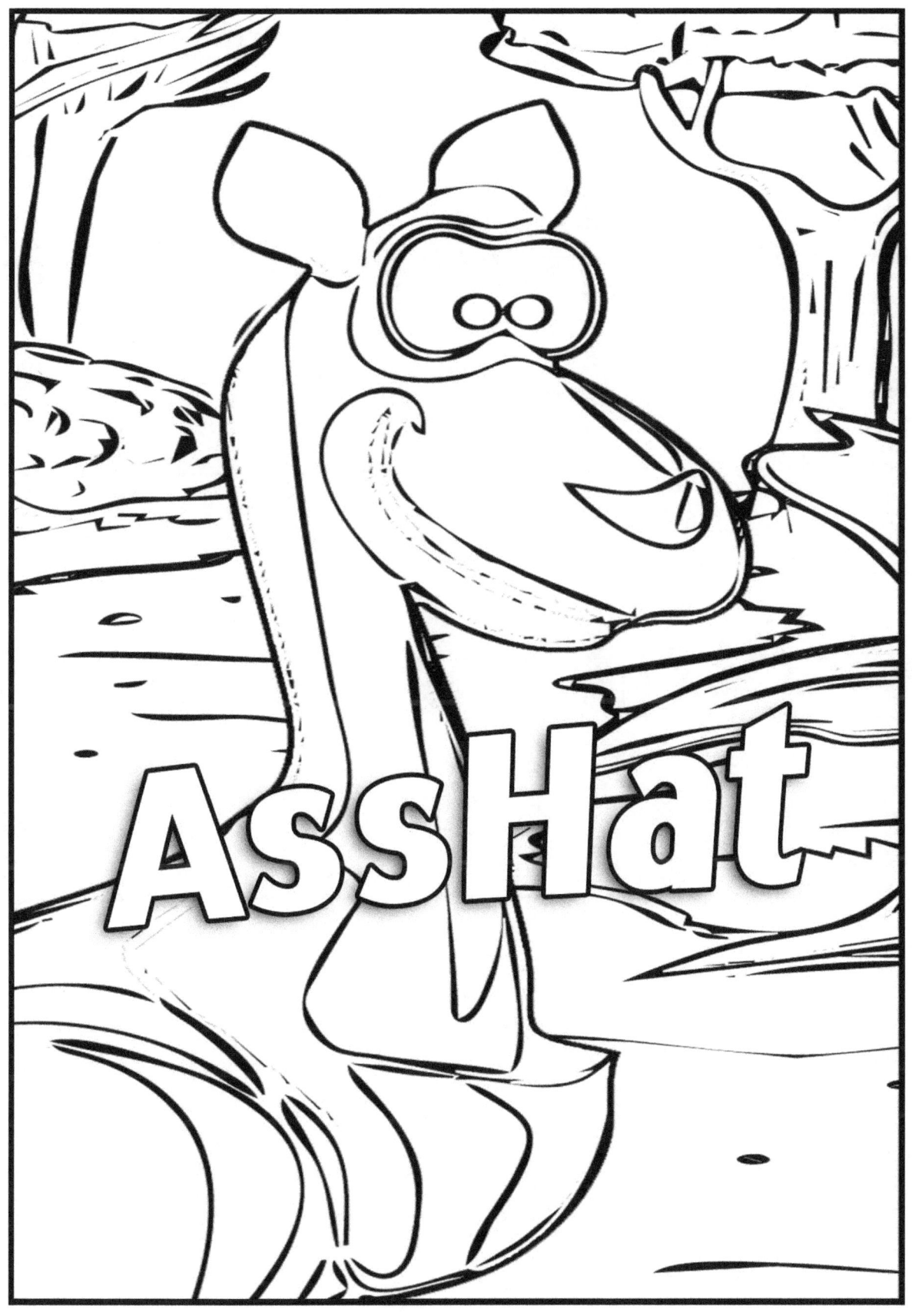

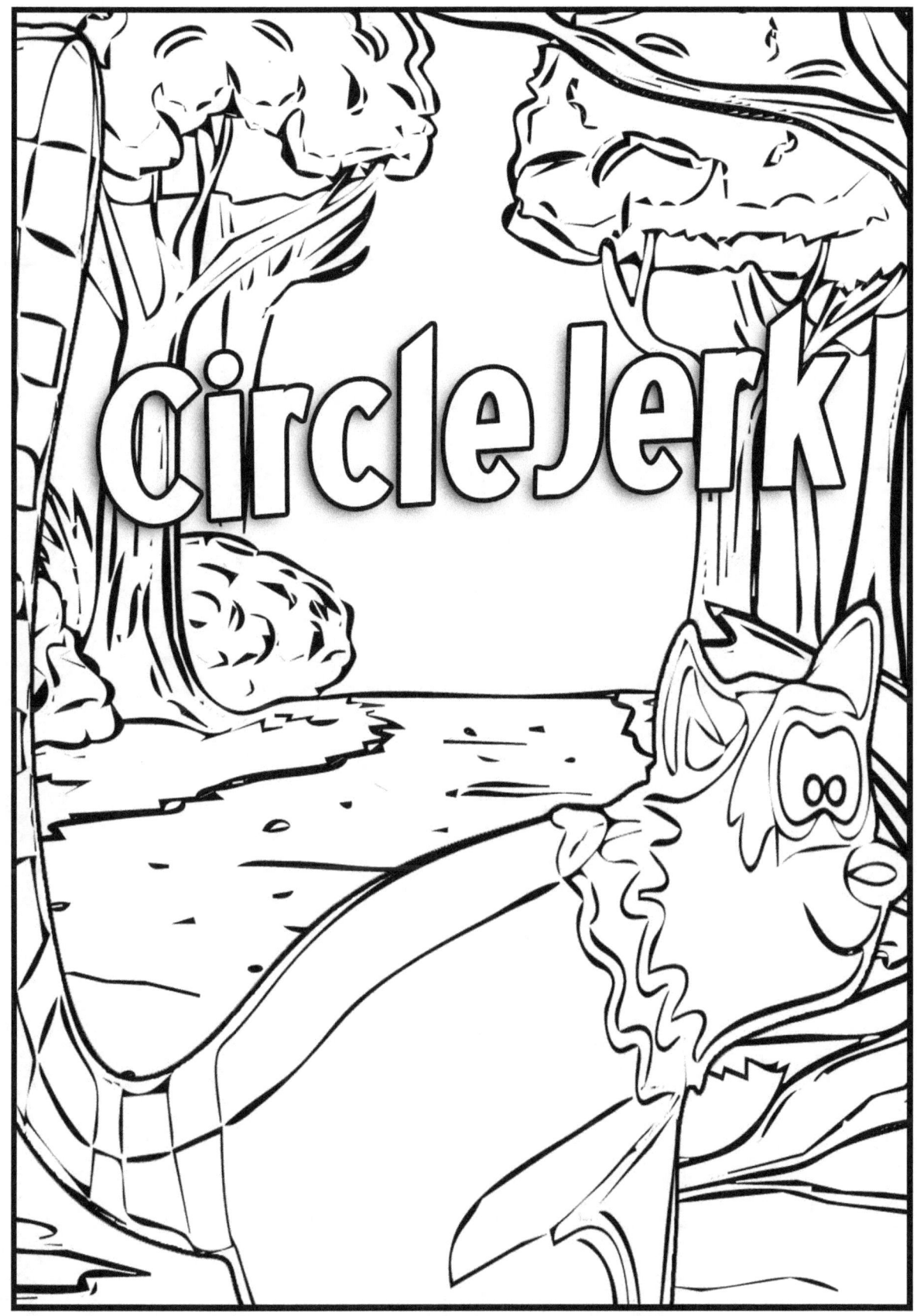

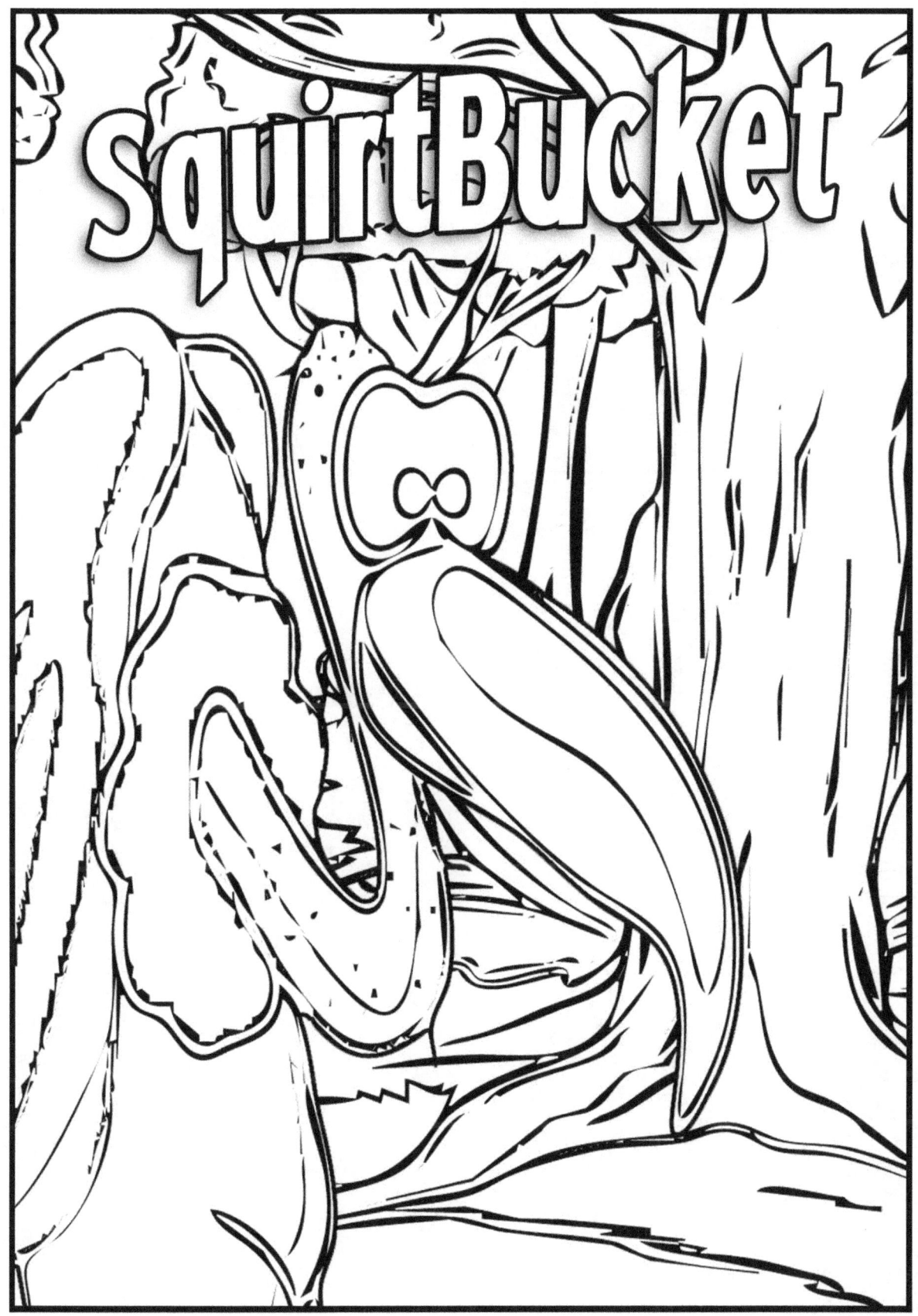

www.ingramcontent.com/pod-product-compliance
Lightning Source LLC
Chambersburg PA
CBHW080611190526
45169CB00007B/2973